Forester

For the wilderness in all of us

Jim Brennan

ISBN 0-9737585-0-3

1. Fiction/Fantasy/Contemporary 2. Photography/Subjects & Themes/Plants & Animals I. Title

The paperback edition is published under ISBN 1-41204103-1

Library and Archives Canada

The complete cataloguing record can be obtained by visiting: http://www.collectionscanada.ca/amicus/index-e.html

Printed in Hong Kong

Dzyngel Productions Inc.
2 Appledore Lane
Stratford, PE
C1B 2P9

www.featherstudio.com

9 8 7 6 5 4 3 2

Contents

Cranky Bear

Highway havoc

It is a beautiful spring day in the Woods. Birds are singing and water is moving again after a long winter's freeze. The cool, crisp air carries the good news from bud to leaf to nose, awakening everything it touches. The most majestic trees to the tiniest flowers are filled with hope. Everyone and everything is celebrating.

Everyone and everything with the exception of Forester, that is. Forester is a bear. He is a bear that did not have a good hibernation. He was restless. His body temperature hardly dropped a degree let alone to a comfortable bear-sleeping-temperature. Before he knew it, spring and incredible hunger pangs called him from his den. He had spent the entire winter tossing and turning and all for one reason – the new highway. Just the thought of that Ribbon of Darkness makes him cranky. It robbed him of his revitalizing sleep. That black-topped ribbon of headless turtles never stopped making noise throughout the entire winter. It was a horrible noise. It was unnatural. It was painful. It's still there! It gobbled up the winter peace and now it is gnawing away at spring. It is as if the headless turtles' feet are on fire, but they can't stop or even slow down. As if they are driven by something. Something evil. Something that doesn't want to let them stop. Something that doesn't know how to stop. A form of madness, maybe. Even when the snow gave everyone a break to enjoy the silence and a moment of being themselves, bigger, shiny headless turtles with great shovels soon came and pushed the snow off the cold, ugly ribbon so the heartless creatures could continue making those painful noises. The sound is awful. It never stops day or night.

He knew the previous summer something was happening. He could hear the work being done on the highway just three hundred winnies from his den. At that time, he thought it was none of his business, but that has all changed. Now it certainly is his business. It is affecting his bearness. He can not permit it. How can he stop it?

What's a bear to do? What's a bear to do? A bear's job is to sleep in the winter. That's what a bear's to do. And eat. Bears must eat. Those are the cornerstones of beardom. He had never had these thoughts before. He knows they are deep thoughts. They must be if it took him this long to have them. He is a bear, after all. He thinks of everything. Forester's head is now ringing with ideas. Ideas that never existed before. He thought: "If a bear doesn't eat and sleep, is he a bear?" Forester rushes to protect himself from these runaway thoughts "I eat, I slept, I think; therefore, I am a bear." After a brief lull of an unknown nature, his logical conclusion helps Forester relax. He shudders a bit as he gets away from where his mind has taken him. He looks around to see if anything has changed. He calms himself, scratches his bear butt and starts to whistle. Then he remembers he can't whistle.

Forester walks over to the place he traditionally visits the first day of spring. It has the earliest growth of fresh new vegetation. He sits. He munches. The shoots are always tasty. They are not, however, tasty enough to take his mind off his situation. He thinks. He picks a shoot and pulls it between his teeth. The juicy, wet pulp falls on his tongue and he swallows. He does not smile as he always does when he eats the tasty shoots. His mind is elsewhere.

After much thought, Forester realizes the puzzling situation is really very simple. It only has two outcomes: Either the Ribbon of Darkness or Forester has to go. Forester is very quick minded about such issues. The ribbon has to go. He doesn't mind where it goes as long as he can't hear it. Or smell it. He doesn't know what the headless turtles eat, but they have an awful stink. Whatever they are guzzling it must be very, very old. It should probably not be eaten at all. The biggest ones belch great, blue puffs and then groan in pain.

Forester thinks some more. He wants to be fair. He prides himself on being a fair bear. He decides that, if he is going to consider himself a fair bear, he should probably be fair. He thinks some more. He has been using this den for hibernation for five glorious years. Five undisturbed, glorious years. In fact, it was the lack of disturbances that made it glorious. That and the comfy way the winter wind blows by the door and the ground supports his back just so. The ribbon has only been in the Woods for one year. Surely it is easier for the headless turtles to move. Where were they before? They can go back There. Maybe they are Here because there is no Back There, back there anymore. Maybe something happened to Back There. He has heard of great areas of trees disappearing practically overnight. He doesn't know if it is true, but it is definitely possible. Bears always know what is possible.

Forester thinks some more. He realizes he is completely responsible for the protection of this den. In fact, the whole den area. This is a responsibility that outweighs most bears' responsibility. He is using the den that Jacob used before him. The great Jacob. The Jacob known throughout the valleys and mountains in all directions for his wisdom and huge appetite. The fact that this is Jacob's chosen spot means it must be protected. This land is sacred, not just to Forester, but to all bears who knew Jacob and the ways of Jacob. It is sacred to all bears everywhere as Jacob embodies the greatness of the Bear Spirit. "Bears," Jacob always said, "are molded in the image of goodness." It would be wrong to forget these wise words. It is important to be fair to the headless turtles, but he also must be good. It's only right. There has only ever been one Jacob. He must be honored. Forester is duty-bound.

Resolute Bear

Bye-bye highway

By combining logical bear-thinking, deductive reasoning and the wise words of Jacob, Forester now knows what he must do. Luckily, what he must do is very easy for a bear. It's natural. He must be fair. Well, that presents no problem. He has already done that. He considered the needs of the headless turtles and the needs of bears. Not everybody considers the other position, so that is unusually fair.

He must be good. Bears are good for goodness' sake. There is no doubt of that. They are molded in the image of goodness. Forester has been good by remembering the wise words of Jacob and using those words in analyzing the needs of those unhappy, screeching creatures.

Forester's conclusion must be correct. He considers all the information, just to be sure.

Well, of course he is correct. He has been fair in considering the other point of view. He has been good in considering all the information, not just the bits that suit him. He must be right if he has been fair and good. What else is there? Oh yes, kindness. Forester must be kind. Well, of course he is kind. Everybody knows he is kind. Sometimes, animals who don't even know him, stare and say very slowly, "WE KNOW YOUR KIND". Forester has always taken great pride in his kindness.

Now he must proceed with all the information he has gathered. He must understand the problem, analyze it, reach a workable solution and implement that solution. Those are the step-by-step procedures in bear problem-solving. Forester remembers the most important step is to make sure he understands the problem. He reviews all of the details. Yup, he understands it. He is ready to move forward.

There are lots of places on the planet that could be used for such ugly creatures as the headless turtles and their questionable habits. Here in the Woods is not one of them.

Forester is pleased with this conclusion and rewards himself with a particularly large, juicy shoot. He collects a paw full of roots to keep the thinking juices flowing.

Here, as in this Here and not some other Here, is too important to be

4

made disgusting by this Here invasion by headless turtles.

Yup. That follows. Forester rubs his paws together excitedly as he falls entirely into the process of problem-solving.

What about There? There's lots of There out there. Jacob often spoke of There. In fact, he was from There. He moved Here for its beauty and calming nature. He said he would never go back There.

Forester fidgets with the success of this realization. He is onto something. The solution is beginning to form.

There sounds like an ideal place for these There creatures. After all, they are from There. Or at least, they must be because they sure aren't from

Here. Not this Here anyway.

A smile crosses Forester's face. The problem is there are There creatures who are becoming Here creatures when they should really remain There creatures. Eureka! He has identified the problem. And he has done it all before lunch.

As Forester paws at the wet ground in search of more roots and shoots, his smile fades. He realizes this is precisely the case of Jacob. Jacob was a There bear before he was a Here bear. He chose to become a Here bear. It is the only case Forester ever considered where bears are not a good example. The analysis simply doesn't work the same when bears are used. Besides, he has made a mistake in the process of problem-solving. He is no longer defining the problem. He is at the analysis stage. He can't keep wandering back. No solution will come of such wishy-washy thinking. Years and years of problem-solving have proven the known method as the best method. As smart as Forester is, this is not something he should change. This, he realizes is a rule. There aren't many bear rules. Just bear bones rules: no living bear can make rules. Rules must evolve naturally. That's the rule. For a proper answer, all that can be considered now is analysis and solution.

This has been a very productive morning, an exhausting and productive morning. It has been a long morning and it is only ten o'clock. Forester is pleased. He has time to go to Crashing Waters. It's a spring thing. Well, actually it is a Forester thing, but he really enjoys it most in the spring. The water crashes louder in the spring. There is more of it and it is in a hurry. The long delay of winter always causes a spring rush.

As Forester approaches Crashing Waters, his heart starts racing with excitement. He likes sitting at the bottom and letting the water pull at his feet. He has an idea. Maybe those screeching headless turtles don't have water to cool their feet. It could be that simple. No. That doesn't explain the horrible smell of them. Well, maybe some of it.

Forester carefully walks over to his favorite place at the bottom of Crashing Waters. The water pulls on his feet. It is just as he remembers it. It is wonderful. He sits on a log. The sound of the water and the coolness of it on his feet helps clear his mind. He should wonder why water on his feet clears his mind, which is so far from his feet, but his mind is too busy being cleared.

When Forester's mind returns, it is refreshed. All the little thinking bits are where they belong and he is ready to start. He considers the problem again. And the solution. There is no sense having a problem if you don't have a solution. Now that he has the solution, he can think more about the problem.

"The headless turtles are unhappy. Oooooh, that's a nice thought. Of course they are unhappy," Forester smiles. "They screech as they zoom down the ribbon, but they never stop moving. That is unhappy. The night comes and their eyes burn with fury. That is unhappy. They go too fast to be anywhere. They are always coming or going on the ribbon. In fact, they are so fast, it seems they are always coming and going at the same time. Where does that leave them?"

He thinks further….

"In my Woods! That's where! In the sacred Woods I must defend for all bearkind!"

Educated Bear

Evil turtles

Forester, armed with his new knowledge and powerful deductive reasoning, heads over to the ribbon to get a better understanding of the enemy. "Well, they are really only enemies if they choose to be enemies. If they just do what's asked of them, they can be friends. We can all be friends," Forester says to himself.

Forester reasons, "They are probably quite smart…although I don't know when they find time to think. How can they think when they are paying so much attention to their comings and goings? Thinking is an inside thing. Paying attention is an outside thing. Thinking and eating go together. They are both inside things. Eating keeps your stomach occupied while your head does the thinking. Thinking and watching or listening are completely incompatible. Together they would require your head to be inside and outside at the same time. An obvious impossibility. Your head would have to be inside-out."

"Head! What head?" He remembers that they don't have heads. "Oh dear!" He may not be able to reason with them at all. Where will he look when he speaks? "Their eyes are in their bellies, but where are their ears? If they don't have heads for thinking, maybe they don't need ears," he reasons.

Ears! If he can locate ears, then what is between them must be a head. Forester dances a few steps on the soft spruce-needle floor as he reflects on his latest accomplishment. He has reduced the impossible to the merely difficult. Difficult things are easy for bears.

So, once their ears are located and their heads deduced, he simply needs to explain the seriousness of the situation to them. "Let's see… 'This land is bear land, not your land; it is sacred. Roaring and screeching in agony at high speed at all hours in all seasons is not respectful in any land. Please go away.'" That should do it. It seems very clear to Forester. If it doesn't work the first time, he will say it again more slowly. And louder. Louder is very important. When they agree to his request, he will ask them for lunch. Forester reflects on lunch. Maybe he won't like what they have for lunch. Maybe inviting them to take a break at Crashing Waters is better. It is more proper. That's it. They can cool and wash their feet.

Forester continues along the path. As he is putting a few final touches on his speech to the headless turtles, the beautiful sound from Crashing

8

Waters fades into the background. Screeches from the Ribbon of Darkness start to drown out all the beautiful sounds of the Woods. The noise makes him feel jittery and his thoughts start bumping together. His thoughts are becoming all crumpled up into one until the only thought remaining is, "Go away!"

Forester locates a nice patch of clover. It is far enough from the gravel and the ribbon to be safe, but close enough to allow for good viewing. It will provide him with light snacks while he studies the enemy. From here he can view their feet and their eyes. He can try to find their ears so he knows exactly where to yell at them. It would be really embarrassing if he yelled into their noses.

Forester settles in to watch and learn. Most of all, he wants to know about their intentions. Forester is very good at watching facial expressions and determining what each expression means. Even the smallest gesture can carry a great deal of weight in deciding his next move.

VROOOOM! The first creature goes by at a roaring clip.

Forester analyzes the data.

The creature was fast. Very, very fast.

It didn't acknowledge him. Okay, he understands that. It must have poor eyesight. That's obvious.

No, wait. If it has poor eyesight, how does it maneuver at such high speeds on such a thin ribbon? It probably has poor eyesight. That's better.

It was red. Not red like a fox, but red like autumn leaves and shiny like fire. It was short like a bush, not tall like a tree. So, it looks like a flying, burning bush. That could explain the screams of pain it gave off and why it doesn't acknowledge him, but not why there are flying, burning bushes tearing back and forth on the ribbon all hours of the day and night. They didn't used to be Here.

Just then a moose wanders out of the Woods. She, too, is enjoying the fresh, new vegetation.

"Hey, Moose!" Forester yells out, "What do you know about these flying, burning bushes?"

The moose replies, "They are tough to eat. I lick them when they are covered in salt, but the nut itself is too hard for my teeth. They have a horrible, metallic taste anyway."

Forester asks, "How do you lick something that is going lickety-split down the ribbon?"

"Oh, avoid them on the ribbon. Only approach them when they are stopped," advises Moose.

"Stopped?" Forester replies, "I didn't know they had a stopped state."

"Oh yeah," replies Moose, "They gather in great clumps a few horizons from here. It is a weird place, I tell you. They have great, tall sticks stuck in the ground to chase away the night. I am not kidding you. Night won't go near the place. And the noise! A girl can't hear herself think!"

"Have you ever tried chasing one?" asks Forester.

"No," says Moose, "but I have been chased by one."

"Wow, how did that work out?" Forester asks, paying full attention.

"No problem," says Moose, "I just got out of its way. They are terrified to leave the ribbon."

Now Forester is really interested. "Why?"

10

Moose rips out a great mouthful of clover, munches on it and swallows before replying. "Because they blow up and burst into flames."

"Oh dear," says Forester. "You have seen this?"

"Not personally, but I know someone who has." Moose turns to go back into the Woods. "See you again, Bear. Be careful."

"I will, and thanks, Moose." Forester stands and stretches. He wonders what he should be careful about. He is a bear. Bears don't have to be careful. It's others that have to be careful.

Forester stands and watches and thinks. What Forester thinks is that he has a respect for these creatures. Scaring away the night, that's pretty scary of them. Then again, they have a fear of not being on the ribbon.

That's it! That is the detail he was missing. If he can get one of them off the ribbon – without blowing it up – it will be more vulnerable and therefore more subject to reason. That is all he has to do. If Forester can convince one of them to go away, then he can surely convince it to tell others of the plan at one of their nightless gatherings. He wishes he had thought of this when they first started moving Here.

Driven Bear

The encounter

Forester watches two more flying, burning bushes go by and then one so big it looks more like a hedge. He is ready to start putting his plan into action. The whole plan is sensitive to size, so he wants to do it before they get any bigger.

His plan is to jump in front of one, forcing it to stop. If it doesn't stop, he will extend the courtesy of standing aside and waiting for it to stop. His backup plan is to do it all again until one of them stops.

Forester steps out onto the ribbon. He feels the surface with his feet. Yuck! No wonder they screech in pain. He feels the ribbon with his paw and scratches it with his claws. It's hard! Even if they need something to guide them, you would think they would prefer to travel beside it on the nice, soft ground.

The ribbon needs more analysis before it can be understood. Forester bends down on all fours and looks for a good spot to sniff. He finds the perfect spot. Well, 'perfect' hardly describes any aspect of this thing, but the best spot for the job. He puts his nose very close to the surface and takes a deep breath. Forester processes the information. The first analysis is ready. The ribbon smells like fire. No, fire doesn't smell; things that burn smell. It smells like something is burning that isn't there. That doesn't make sense. Oh yes it does, if one views it clearly from a completely new perspective. It is the smell of the burning bushes that never stand still long enough to be there.

Forester hears one coming. It is the correct time, he thinks, so it has to be the correct size. What if it isn't the correct size? Well then, he will just have to adjust the data accordingly.

It is coming very fast. Forester stands to one side to allow it enough space to stop, but it is going too fast. It disappears over the hill. That was a good test. The next one is the real one. This may be the most important thing he does in his entire, maybe short, life.

It's coming…It's coming…It's coming…It is stopping! It is even pulling over to the gravel!

Forester's plan is incomplete and as such, it suffers from a lack of detail. He does not know what to do next. He is going to wing it. He walks over to the now-quiet creature. It doesn't so much as blink. On the other hand, what looks to him like four parasites burrowed into it are very excited. While that is mildly interesting, his business is with the creature.

As Forester gets closer, there is a whirring sound and then the parasites start making clicking sounds. There is something wrong here. The parasites seem to be running the show. Forester knows it can feel like that, but he has never known it to be like that. He needs to go away and review the evidence over a few berries. Something is very strange in beardom!

The creature screeches off.

What kind of creature builds a symbiotic relationship with its parasites? Symbiotic? It appears to be more one-sided, really. This isn't a natural state of affairs. Everyone knows parasites have their place, and their place isn't running the show. Forester knows this interesting relationship is the key to his success. He has to understand the relationship. He has been given a tool to use against these creatures. He must learn how to use it.

After a brief lunch, a visit to Crashing Waters, and much reflection on the encounter he has just experienced, Forester returns to the ribbon, refreshed. This time he is going to take more control. He must be assertive. He will be understanding, but very firm. These creatures must go.

A large one is coming. It is big. Very big. Bigger than any bear. It has a clown painted on its side. Forester takes a deep breath and stands in the middle of the ribbon. The creature keeps coming. Surely, the thing will have enough respect for life to avoid hitting him. Forester worries: It is not slowing…It is not changing course! It…It…! "Oh no!" says Forester, "Jacob spoke of clowns and circuses. That is what he ran away from!" He holds his ground, determined to…

Forester jumps onto the gravel just in time to feel the side of the thing slide past his beautiful coat, not to mention all the vital bits that make a bear, a bear. The wind it creates as it whizzes past him is amazing. It makes a small shower of rain. It can control the weather! Forester panics. "It is not safe. It must be stopped. But not this way." Forester is shaken. He looks down the ribbon to see the creature disappear over the horizon. He waits for his legs to stop trembling before standing upright again. Forester has never felt so defeated. He was only going to ask nicely. Jacob was so right. If that was a There creature, Forester is not going There. Ever! They are rude, mean and do not care about anyone or anything. And that ugly clown painted on its side! How can I trust something that looks like that?

Forester heads off into the Woods trying to hold back his emotions. His feelings are hurt. There was no need for that type of behavior. Life as a bear can be difficult enough without unnecessarily difficult encounters to worry about. Forester feels a type of alone he has never felt before. It is as if there isn't enough of him. Or maybe there is too much of him. There is not enough of him to go around the amount of him there is. That's what he knows. That, and it doesn't feel good.

As Forester heads to an extra-special roots and shoots place he saves for very special occasions, he hears two chipmunks in a tree behind him. They are discussing him. They say he is very brave to have stood up to the devil's own creatures. Forester is moved by their kind words. He feels he is a part of something. In fact, he is a part of everything. Everything that matters. Not everyone in the Woods always gets along, but at least they all have their place in it. It is the Woods and he's the bear. So there, Devil-May-Care! He smiles to himself.

Planning Bear

The voice

Forester walks back to a cool, spring pond to enjoy the waters and have a little lunner, his favorite meal between lunch and dinner. As he walks, he feels a light headed and refreshing sensation that happens to him after a terrible event is followed by a joyous one. Joy has so much more room to stretch out and fill a bear that has been left empty by meanness.

Forester sits in the pond eating pond vegetation and sipping cool water. His thoughts are still on the Ribbon of Darkness and the headless turtles. Now more than ever, he realizes the value of his home and the potential threat to it. He realizes he is in need of a good idea. No, a good idea is not good enough. He needs a great idea. As Forester sits in the pond searching through his mind for the perfect great idea, a particularly large mosquito lands on his ear. Without thinking, at least not about his ear, he reaches up and slaps the side of his head very hard. At that moment or a second or two later, Forester is not certain, a voice comes to him. "You cannot fight this monster alone, Forester. You must get all the animals to help you."

Forester looks around for the source of the voice before realizing it wasn't that sort of voice. Being unfamiliar with the proper etiquette for such a situation and still feeling a bit dizzy from the slap, he is uncertain if he should respond out loud or to himself. Should he address the voice or should it be a general comment? As the voice did not introduce itself, it is probably a fairly open forum. He knows in all situations a response is correct, so he speaks out loud. And as he is right here, he is sure to hear it as well.

"Voice," Forester starts, "why would my neighbors help. They fear me."

"No, Forester," replies the voice calmly, "they respect you."

Forester takes a moment and then decides. It is best not to argue with such a wise voice.

When it is just a voice, it is hard to know when the conversation is over, so, to be sure, Forester waits without saying anything. He lies down completely covered by water except for the very tip of his nose. The water protects him from mosquitoes and allows him to have a wonderfully fresh bath while he waits and wonders. He stares up through the water to the beautiful blue sky and thinks about how he can turn respect into action. He has a mission and it is to get rid of the ribbon creatures. It is important to all animals of the Woods. His neighborhood is plagued by the headless turtles and he has been chosen for his brilliant bear mind to protect it. He will apply himself to the problem entirely until it has been solved.

It is almost quarter after mealtime when Forester rises from the water. He has never been so late for anything in his whole life. But food? Something's afoot. He couldn't feel better. He has never been this clean before. Not only does he have a good home and neighborhood, he has a mission. A reason to be. Something that reaches beyond him. It even reaches beyond beardom. It will benefit the entire animal kingdom. This is better than berries. Forester stops and ponders that thought, but does not reach a conclusion before moving on to thoughts of organizing the neighborhood. "Wow," he realizes, "that's a big job! That's a bear of a job!" That job has his name all over it!

Forester realizes he should get some shoots and roots into him. It is important to be well fed when planning. If there is one thing he has learned about planning, it is the importance of not being disturbed. He doesn't want his belly talking to his brain when his brain is trying to work. He will eat enough now so his belly has plenty of work of its own. If he eats enough, his belly will be far too busy to bother his brain.

After giving his belly enough work to keep it occupied until dinner, he makes a list. The first thing he must do is call a meeting. That will not be easy. To his knowledge, it has never been done before. He needs to talk to representatives of different groups and ask them to attend the meeting. So, even before the first thing he must do, he must talk to as many animals of as many species as he can and tell them of the meeting. Okay. That will be the very first thing. Forester is pleased with his progress. He has just started and already he has two items of business clearly identified. Forester reviews his plan: very first thing, tell everyone about the meeting; first thing, hold a meeting. Oh, oh! He must figure out where to hold the meeting before talking to everyone or holding a meeting. That's no problem.

Forester is happy. Three items are already defined. This is progress, an event in the making. It is a good time to review his plan. The very, very first item is to find a location for the meeting, the very first item then is to talk to as many animals as possible about the meeting, then and only then, when the other two items are complete, can he do the first thing, which is to hold the meeting. Forester is one gifted bear. His organization skills are outstanding. He is a clear thinker and a creative thinker at the same time. This ribbon thing could work out to be good for the entire Woods. It could draw everyone together to reap the great benefits of beardom.

Forester thinks about first talking to other bears before going ahead and telling everyone the inner secrets of bears. Although bears never promise to keep secret the rules of Bearology, Bearstory, Bearmatics or any of the other classical learning methods, these rules have never before been shared. On the other hand, the ribbon changed the rules. Bears must see a new path. A path that includes everyone. Except, of course, the ignorant and mean ribbon runners.

Savvy Bear

The plan

Forester decides to sleep by the river where everyone comes to drink. It is quiet and allows him to think clearly. In the early morning light, three deer approach and start drinking. Forester, who is behind a few small bushes stands, clears his throat and starts to speak softly, but with a sense of importance. The three deer jump back, startled.

"Oh, don't be afraid," Forester says kindly, "I mean you no harm."

"We didn't know you could speak kindly," the biggest deer says.

"Bears speak many languages," Forester replies as gently as a bear can. He takes a small breath for timing. "We are a reserved creature, choosing to speak only when it is important. It is a sign of wisdom. Bear is a difficult language to learn but a wonderful language for advancing ideas, so we tend to speak Bear to each other. We learn other languages to speak with other animals."

"Bear is most likely quite sufficient for bears," the youngest deer replies, turning back to drink more water.

"You seem to have something on your mind, Bear. What is it?" asks the biggest deer.

"You have probably noticed a new evil lurking in the Woods over the last few months," Forester starts to say.

"If you are talking about those dreadful, gigantic headless turtles that appear to be something from the Palaeolithic period, I haven't noticed them lurking too much. They move at a reckless speed, hissing and screeching in what I take for some reptilian language based neither on politeness nor intelligence." the biggest deer replies.

"Yes, I think we are talking about the same thing," says Forester.

"You have a plan?" asks the biggest deer.

"Well… yes" says Forester, slowly.

"What is your plan?" asks the biggest deer.

"I have given it a great deal of thought and I think we need to make a plan," says Forester.

"That is your plan?" The biggest deer stares at Forester in curiosity.

"Yes. Do you have a better one?" asks Forester.

"No," replies the biggest deer.

"Then my plan is the best plan," says Forester firmly.

"So it is." says the biggest deer. The little deer groans and rolls her eyes.

The biggest deer continues. "How do you want to go about making this plan?"

"Well, I thought we could start by getting everybody together," says Forester.

"Oh, right you are," says the middle deer. "We can have a buffet after. That will help attract the cougars and the wolves. They will go anywhere for a free meal OF VENISON! They make pigs of themselves at our expense and then joke about the fast food not being quite fast enough. Uggggh! Evil creatures!"

"Just once we must put our little differences aside. It is more important that we consider the future of all animalkind than just our own selfish complaints. All could be lost and then where would we be?" asks Forester.

"Is that rhetorical?" the middle deer asks as she returns to drinking.

"The bear has a point," the big deer says. "We were all there that horrible night Glades was so brutally killed. The worst part was the headless turtle didn't even stop to eat her. It just left her on the side of the ribbon, in the prime of her life. She went down the food chain, not up. It was all so horrible! And the fawns! Oh, the fawns! We must act if the natural order is to be preserved."

"So the plan is in place. Long live the plan!" enthuses Forester, pounding his fist into the air and thumping his foot.

"What is the next step?" asks the middle deer.

"We must call everyone together. I will speak with the carnivores, unless of course you happen to see them first; you can ask all the herbivores but I think it is very important once we gather that everyone should mingle. There is no sense having a group divided from the start. We will never get anywhere unless we work together." Forester counsels.

"Right then, shall we all meet at Babbling Brook Hollow the day following two misty mornings?" Forester recommends with authority.

"What time?" asks the biggest deer.

"Oh, this time is good. It will give us an early start." replies Forester.

"Hey! You there, squirrel in the dead spruce, can you get all the squirrels to attend?" Forester calls.

"Okee dokee," replies the squirrel.

"Just tell them it is a meeting for the common good. That should do it," says Forester.

"I will tell them the cougars and the deer will be meeting," the squirrel said, running off. "That's what will do it."

With everything started, Forester realizes he had better have something to eat. As he walks, he reflects on the wonderful gift he is giving all the other animals, the wisdom of Beardom. Everyone will learn to hibernate and let the Woods regenerate in the wintertime. Everyone will be able to discuss lofty ideas in the language of Bear. Well, Quick Bear. They will never grasp Ponder Bear or heaven forbid, Idea Bear. The very thought of a deer speaking Idea Bear makes Forester laugh. "They are my neighbors and I love them, but they are ideal neighbors, not idea neighbors. They will never understand even the little things bears understand, but they will be able to ask bears for advice." He will be able to tell them how to locate the best shoots. No, it might be better if they develop certain abilities on their own. Food is very important and must be managed correctly. Bears know that for sure.

Honey is too rich for other animals even in small doses. It doesn't take much honey for a bear to have some very powerful thoughts. There would be no safe amount for a rabbit or a hare. Who knows what hare-brained schemes they might come up with if they knew the power of honey? It is best no one else be told about it. Bears would be forever responsible if honey became the root of all evil.

After his mid-mid-morning snack, Forester goes to Babbling Brook Hollow where the great meeting will be held. It is perfect. It has just the right slope. There is plenty of space for ground animals and trees for tree animals. Let's not forget about birds. They will make wonderful lookouts. Particularly crows. Boy, are they nosey! They miss nothing. And do they love to gossip. Well, ribbon guarding will give them something to talk about.

Leader Bear

The meeting

The day of the big meeting arrives. Trees are filled with birds, squirrels, chipmunks and raccoons all wanting the best view. The ground is covered with deer, rabbits, foxes, porcupines, weasels, rats, groundhogs and many, many other animals including bears. Skunks are gathered over to one side, but no one takes offense to their standoffishness. There is a cougar on the bank on either side of the river. They are very particular not to step into each other's territory. Forester stands on a stump, looking about to ensure

everyone has a great view of him. He chose the stump yesterday and dragged it into position specifically for the purpose. On either side of him stands a very proper black bear watching and waiting for Forester to start.

"First, I want to welcome everyone to Babbling Brook Hollow for what promises to be the most important meeting ever." Forester says looking about the audience appearing to speak to everyone individually. He knows that is very important.

On top of an enormous tree on one side of the great hollow, a crow is heard to say, "Being as this is the first meeting, that is a fairly safe proclamation for you to make."

Forester continues on his mission without acknowledging the crow's comment, "If you leave this meeting with only one thought, let it be the importance of the expulsion of the ribbon runners from our home! It is a gargantuan task. A task so large as to require the wisdom and strength of beardom."

As Forester performs, the bears to his left and right look up to him listening in awe and nodding in agreement at key moments.

Bears, strategically located throughout the crowd, clap and cheer after every important point.

"Yes, dear friends, bears everywhere have realized the need for the greater good to prevail. We are going to share our vast knowledge built up over hundreds of bird visits and snow-filled winters. Knowledge carefully considered over many uninterrupted winters." Forester's face wrinkles with memories of the past winter. His attempts at disguising his anger fail. "Winters now cluttered up by ribbon runners and their noise!" Forester focuses on the positive to regain control. He takes a deep breath and pauses to divide the good news from the bad. He smiles. "We are giving everyone, regardless of their importance in the natural order, the benefits of beardom.

"Beardom will prevail!" pours out the chant from the bears. "Beardom will prevail!"

Forester's popularity quickly becomes whelming and then rockets to overwhelming. It is not so much the message, but the way Forester says it. He has stage presence. He has a stage. He is a one-bear marvel! He turns those foul-smelling ribbon creatures into the devil's own scourge. He does it all with words. Common words. Infectious words. Motivating words. Words thrown to the left. Words thrown to the right. Waves of emotion carry everyone off to a land where everything is possible and everybody is included. No easy chore, considering bears often speak of bad personal traits in terms unbecoming to some of the members of the audience, such as rats and weasels. But these foul-smelling creatures are worse than any rat or weasel could ever be. And besides, rats and weasels are friends now. Forester never slips. He is in the moment.

Everyone, with the exception of the birds, is squarely behind him and his plan. As the meeting advances, it is revealed that some birds are harvesting road-kill and don't want to give up this important part of their livelihood. It is further established that all other birds feel it is in their best interest for all birds to vote as a group.

"If I could speak of an old raccoon tradition at this time, I would feel most privileged," says a large, older raccoon sitting with a few other raccoons.

"I am certain no one here is too busy for a few brief words from a raccoon," says Forester.

Forester feels the crowd drift a bit as they moan collectively under their breath. He will use levity to bring them back. "LIGHTEN UP! Raccoons are close relative of bears, so what they have to say is relative." Forester smiles. Alone.

"We use a method called 'pebbles and ripples' when raccoonity loses cohesion, " Raccoon continues. "What's that?" the crowd replies in bored unison.

"Pebbles and ripples?" Raccoon asks with excitement.

"No," is the reply. "Cohesion."

"Unity," says Raccoon, a little worried he is losing them. "If a raccoon feels the greater raccoon good is in jeopardy, a clam hunt is called. Attendance is voluntary. The first one to find a clam leads all others to Mirror Lake. Once everyone is gathered, he gently tosses a pebble into the middle of the lake. Those in attendance watch the ripples."

"Great idea," says Forester. "Now then… if we meet…."

"I have just started," says Raccoon, irritably.

"I apologize," says Forester with a voice of tolerant impatience.

Raccoon continues, "Anyone wanting to comment on an issue tosses a pebble. The location of the new pebble and the size and pattern of the ripples allow everyone to see if the response agrees or disagrees and to what degree."

26

"How do you know what you are casting pebbles about?" asks a skunk.

"Oh, everybody knows the issues and which issues are causing the most problems," replies Raccoon "Everybody knows where everyone else stands on every issue and which issues are most important to them, so knowing which issue or what the first pebble represents is not an issue."

"That is very good," says Skunk. "We usually get bogged down or start arguing when we try defining the issue."

Raccoon smiles and then continues, "Further opinions lead to further pebble tosses. The pebbles and ripples method allows everyone a voice and to see the collective voice without raising a voice or having to listen to time-stealing bragging. One opinion is as valid as another. Nothing is hidden in words. If fact, no one is allowed to speak. When it is over, everyone knows what to do."

"How do you know when it is over?" asks a fox.

"There are no more tossed pebbles and no more ripples," replies Raccoon, patiently.

"What if someone throws a great, large rock?" asks a bear.

"Yah," says a rat, "what if someone pelts the lake with all kinds of pebbles?"

"We are," says Raccoon, disgusted with the questions, "raccoons. We exercise self-control. There is no one else to do that for us."

A porcupine clears her throat and says, "I don't think you solve any problems. Watching all those ripples just makes everyone relax and they don't care about the problem anymore."

"If everyone forgets there is a problem, is there a problem?" another raccoon asks the porcupine.

"Either way, that is not a problem for us. If an afternoon sitting by the lake watching ripples makes us forget our problems, that is solution enough," says an old raccoon, sitting down in the front.

"Do you have to toss a pebble?" asks a little voice in the crowd.

"No. In fact, some issues only attract one pebble toss," replies Raccoon.

"Then that raccoon would be given complete control!" says the little voice.

"That's true," says Raccoon, "but then he may be the only one to watch the ripples."

"How do you read the ripples?" asks a deer.

"They are read holistically rather than analytically," answers Raccoon "Peaks add together to make larger peaks, peaks and valleys cancel each other. Near pebbles make for big ripples, far pebbles make for little ripples."

"What if raccoons really care, but they can't make up their minds," asks the little voice.

"There is lots of time to think and toss... but it happens. It happens to everyone sometimes. You just have to hope you are clearer thinking other times," replies Raccoon.

"What if you can never make up your mind?" says the little voice.

"Oh, a permanently indecisive raccoon," says Raccoon. "I am afraid that has a different solution."

"Do tell," says Rat.

"Well, it seems the good cougars, ever determined to protect us from disease and famine prefer the taste of indecisive raccoon." A bead of sweat forms on Raccoon's brow as he looks towards the bigger cougar sitting on the river bank. "No offense, cougar."

"None taken," says the cougar as he lazily looks at the sky to see what the weather may bring.

"What keeps everybody from tossing their pebbles at the same time?" asks the fox.

"There is an old raccoon expression; 'The age of the opinion can always be told by the timing of the toss.' The young tend to toss early; that has a more immediate influence, but the old wait, knowing the later the toss, the longer the effects."

There is a silence followed by applause, for there is much to be done and everyone is pleased Raccoon has finished speaking.

"That is a nice story, Raccoon," Forester says. "It is probably a good idea to have every species tell a story at a meeting."

Forester continues, "What raises us above common animals is...if I may borrow Raccoon's word...cohesion. We will go forth with common goals, common beliefs and very common ideas. We will fight our enemies where we find them…be it on the ribbon, in the waters or in the sky. We will use the power tools of beardom. We will remain open to the possibility other animals can bring worthy ideas to the group."

Forester looks over at Raccoon: "Why... Raccoon's little story helped us all better understand what we have and what we have to protect. We will make sure no pebble is left untossed in our pursuit of goodness."

Forester surveys the crowd in silence with a great broad smile and then says, " No animal can undo the goodness that has been done here today. We have the headless turtles on the run!"

"Let's all meet again two days after the next day of rain," he says.

The crowd leaves. There is conversation and muttering in all directions as each heads off in his own direction. The deer leave with huge leaps into the Woods while the cougars lollygag. The general mood is very good. It seems Forester and beardom have saved the day.

Supreme Bear

The organization

There is excitement as the second meeting gets started. This time, the animals arrive by species and stand as species. It is all very orderly. The little ones (that can't climb trees) are down in front. The bigger the animal, the farther back they stand. It is truly a miracle to see such community. It is a magnificent communion of the animal kingdom. A celebration of Oneness. The only animals that stand separate are the cougars, once again on either bank. They give each other a courteous nod on arrival. The chipmunks start singing, "Bees do it, Birds do it..." and everyone joins in. One of the cougars starts to smile, but catches himself and stops immediately.

Forester stands on the stump and looks over the large crowd.

"We are gathered here in this magnificent Woods," Forester smiles, reaches out with his palms held high, a stick in his right hand, and turns for all the audience to see him, "to work together to protect ourselves from the new evil that has invaded our lands."

A chipmunk way up in the mightiest pine yells out, "Let's all sing something to celebrate!"

Forester smiles up at the chipmunk and says, "We can sing later, my friend, but first we must discuss our good works. The works that will guide us and our children through this dangerous world. The time has come to show everyone the power of beardom!"

Forester looks over the entire gathering in silence with his paws at rest in front of him. "I would like to ask at this time that everyone save their comments and questions to the end so order can be maintained." Forester laughs a laugh too light to be taken seriously, "If we all speak at once, no one will be heard. I think you will want to hear what some of the other bears and I have come up with to fight the evil that has infected our Woods with screeches and hisses all hours of the day and night."

Forester's face wrinkles into anger as he strikes the stick in his right hand with his left fist. It really emphasizes his message.

"It may be just noise to you," a raccoon yells out, "but you are a great, big bear. For the rest of us, it's our lives. It is the lives of our family and friends that are at stake here. They kill us with no apparent reason. There is little warning."

The skunks look on, nodding their heads in solemn agreement.

"We have addressed that very issue, Brother Raccoon. May I call you 'Brother'?" Forester asks, without waiting for an answer.

"Where are you getting these ideas?" Rat asks.

"I am sorry," says Forester. "I couldn't see who asked the question, but the answer is the same for all. A voice came to me while I was sitting in the spring pond."

"Oh dear," a deer whispers to her friend. "That was my favorite drinking hole. Until now."

"Have you been getting enough natural sugar in your diet?" Rat asks.

"I am a bear," says Forester irritably "What do you know of bears?"

"I know you sleep all winter while the rest of us have to work," a small voice says.

"Precisely. Bears get done in a few months what it takes some other animals a full cycle of bird visits to complete. Wouldn't you all like a little more time off?" asks Forester.

"The bear is right. The bear is right." Voices start to chant.

The bears on either side of the stump start chanting the reply, "Beardom! Beardom!"

Slowly the whole crowd joins in, with the exception of the cougars. The cougars yawn and look about. The big one rests his head on his paws and watches.

(If any humans happen to be reading this story, it is worth noting at this time that a cougar never wears a watch and would not even consider wearing watches. They always know the time and that jewelry would simply detract from their stunning good looks.)

Forester speaks over the chant, "I know you all want to be bears, but that is not possible."

The crowd goes quiet.

"What is possible," he continues, "is for every single one of you to benefit from being an associate member of beardom."

"Can I sleep all winter?" asks a young bunny close to the stump.

"You can do anything you believe," Forester says, looking out over the audience with a smile that starts and ends at his lips.

"How?" asks Bunny.

"Believe enough!" says Forester now looking straight at Bunny.

"I believe enough," says Bunny, silly with the excitement of being noticed by Forester.

"And you must follow the bear ways," says Forester firmly.

"Bear ways," says Rat. "How do we know these bear ways work?"

"Look at me," Forester says looking at everyone but Rat. "Is this not proof enough?" Forester holds out his mighty chest and flexes his muscles.

"I don't want to be big," says Bunny, "I just want to sleep all winter."

"Then you don't have to believe as much as a bear does," says Forester.

"Wow! I only have to believe as much as I want?" says Bunny, excitedly.

"It is even better," Forester says softly, looking down at Bunny. "You only get what you believe in."

Forester starts to address the crowd again. "We have a lot to cover today. Let's start by discussing the rules of beardom and how they can help us defeat our enemies."

"Last week, the fox was my enemy. How do I know who will be my enemy next week?" yells a squirrel from a tree.

"Behold the miracle!" says Forester, "The plan is already working! Those who were enemies at our first meeting are now friends." Forester looks to the sky and holds his hands up in praise, "And we have only just begun."

"Hold up there, big guy," says a deer. "It is no secret that carnivores eat meat. For those of you who may not realize it, we are that meat. That will never change. What about you, cougar? Do you see change soon?"

"Nope," purrs the cougar. "Who am I to question the ways of nature?"

"Yah, bear," a wolf barks. "Your plans seem a little misguided when viewed from the bigger picture."

"Look," says Forester, "all I am asking is that wolves and cougars and other carnivores make a slight change in their eating habits. It is not big. All you have to do is eat berries and roots rather than rabbits and deer."

"Yah," snarls another wolf. "Why don't you work all winter, you big lazy lug?"

Forester knows things are not going well.

"Fish?" Forester asks the wolf again. "Eat fish. Nobody cares about fish."

"I do," howls the wolf. "I…DON'T…LIKE…IT!"

"How do you know?" responds Forester.

"I've been down on my luck," whines the wolf. "I may look like Mister Lucky now, but I know what it's like to be hungry."

"Yah," yells a deer. "Do you know what it is like to be a deer? Constantly having to defend herself and her family from you! You can't imagine."

"You don't understand," says the smaller cougar.

"You bet I don't!" yells the deer.

"Friends, friends, all! Please, please, can we have a little civility? Do you know what is at stake here?" Forester pleads with the crowd. "I can lead you to the land of honey."

The big, black bear on the right taps Forester's side. "Hey, Forester," he whispers, "ixnay on the honey promo. We agreed it could lead to havoc in the hands of common creatures."

"Honey, did I say, honey?" Forester stutters, "It's an endearment. I meant it as an endearment. A place where love prevails and we greet each other as 'Honey'."

"Do you think for one second I would greet that low life over there as 'Honey'?" the deer yells out. "I am disgusted! I am leaving!"

"So am I," says another voice.

As quick as you can imagine it, Babbling Brook Hollow is empty. Even the cougars are gone. Forester is all alone. His noble idea is in ruins.

Worldly Bear

The after-shock

The summer passes. The headless turtles continue screeching up and down the ribbon. Forester visits Babbling Brook Hollow and stands alone on the stump, still trying to understand what happened. Even the two most faithful bears left him without a word. He steps down, takes a few steps, and then looks back at his stump. He sighs and walks off in the direction of his den. Bunny comes hopping out from behind a tree.

"You know," says Bunny, "nobody proved you wrong."

Forester keeps walking with slumped shoulders and, without turning, says, "They didn't have to. I did that on my own."

"So," says Bunny, "have you never been wrong before?"

"I never invited everybody from everywhere to watch me perform it before," replies Forester.

"You are just feeling sorry for yourself. I do that sometimes. I find it helps," says Bunny, kindly.

Forester doesn't reply.

"Are you angry?" asks Bunny.

"My mother taught me that anger is useless," explains Forester. "It happens, but it is useless. It is just what you do when you try to wrestle control away from The-Way-It-Is."

"Who is The-Way-It-Is?" asks Bunny.

"Who is The-Way-It-Is? Oh my goodness, Bunny! The-Way-It-Is is who makes it the way it is!" exclaims Forester.

"I thought everybody makes it the way it is," Bunny replies.

"We all play a part, Bunny, but The-Way-It-Is does it when we are not," says Forester.

"Not what?" Bunny asks, still not understanding.

"Making it the way it is," explains Forester.

"Oh. That makes sense. I guess I just never thought about it," says Bunny.

"You didn't need to. You are not a bear, Bunny," replies Forester with a smile.

"So where are you going?" asks Bunny.

"I am going to my den. It is bedtime," replies Forester, yawning.

"Bedtime?" Bunny says enthusiastically.

Forester stops and looks at Bunny. "Do you want to join me?"

"Oh my, yes!" says Bunny. "That would be marvelous. Do you mind if I hop out for a bite now and then?"

"No, that will be all right," Forester says smiling at Bunny. "That is all part of being Bunny isn't it?"

Bunny, smiling up at Forester, can't help but look at his great, big, luxuriant coat: "You know something, Forester, you were right."

"What do you mean?" Forester asks, puzzled.

"Well...you said if I believed enough, I could sleep through the winter," Bunny replies.

Forester smiled down at Bunny.

"I believe enough. I know I do!" says Bunny.

"I still wasn't right," sighs Forester.

"You were right for you and that is as right as right gets," Bunny says, comforting the big bear.

Forester and Bunny keep walking, knowing they are right for each other.

It is a particularly beautiful winter. There is so much snow, the noise of the ribbon is lost in the drifts. Mostly.

Forester sleeps. Oh, how he sleeps! Bunny snuggles up to Forester because they are such good friends. That big, luxuriant coat is very warm as well. Once, when Bunny hops out for something to eat, Forester wakes and looks out and sees Bunny's tracks in the snow. He knows Bunny will not have gone far…just out searching for a little bedtime snack. When Bunny returns, Forester pretends to be asleep. He does it so well, he starts to snore and doesn't stop until spring.

It is funny about Bunny and that snore. The snore is louder than the ribbon runners ever were and Bunny is right beside it. It is not an attractive sound. In fact, some would complain. They wouldn't even have to be close. But not Bunny. It's a wonderful sound to Bunny. It is the sound of friendship. The wonderful, comforting sound of friendship.

Understanding Bear

Beautiful spring

It is a beautiful spring day. Bunny is hopping around outside the den when Forester peers out the door for the first time. His eyes are practically glued shut, he has been sleeping so hard. "Wow!" Forester says, "It's so beautiful! I slept like a bear."

"So did I," says Bunny, "a hungry bear. I gathered some things for you. But you didn't wake up, so I ate them."

"That is okay," replies Forester, "I have my regular bear things to do in the spring. It wouldn't seem like spring without them."

"Oh, Forester, you are celebrating beardom! That's wonderful!" Bunny hops around him excitedly.

"Yes, Bunny. I think it is important bears celebrate beardom. Celebrating beardom in my own special way is what makes me a bear," Forester says.

Forester smiles at Bunny. "Is there bunnydom?"

"Not exactly," says Bunny, very enthusiastic to speak about it. "We have bunnyocity. It is like beardom, but for bunnies. It explains everything from the way a bunny sees it."

"Oh, like when we walk down the road together. You say something as seen by a bunny using bunnyocity, and then I reply as a bear using beardom," Forester says, looking at Bunny.

"Yes," says Bunny stopping on the path, "Let me show you. Close your eyes and we will think together. This won't show you bunnyocity, but if you believe, it will show you the bunny point of view."

"Wow!" says Forester. "That is very different. Do you want to try for the bear point of view?"

"Yes, Forester, I really do," replies Bunny.

"Close your eyes and I will look down the path," says Forester.

"Wow, you can see so far ahead! Now when you say something based in beardom, I will have a better idea of what you are talking about," Bunny says.

When Bunny's eyes open, she sees a cougar heading towards them on the path.

"It is a good thing that when my eyes were closed, yours were open, Forester," Bunny says.

"That is what friends are for, Bunny," Forester says protectively.

As the cougar approaches, Bunny moves over against Forester and says, "Good morning."

To their amazement, the cougar says, "Lovely morning."

"Cougar," Bunny continues, "Forester and I were just comparing life as a bear and life as a bunny."

"And I suppose you want to know more about living life as an amazing cougar?" Cougar purrs.

"Or just as a plain cougar will do," Forester adds.

"Where should I start? You would probably like to know about our innermost thoughts, but that would be quite impossible. You see, cats are very smart, particularly cougars. Our thoughts are too complex for...." Cougar begins to explain.

"I want to know why you eat meat," interrupts Bunny.

"Oh, that...." says cougar with a discouraging tone.

He continues, "That is one reason why cougars are misunderstood by so many other animals. It is a simple matter of physics. We can not be held responsible for the lack of knowledge in other species. If prey only understood quantum physics, there would be no questions."

The question, "Quantum physics?", is stated loudly and clearly by the other two without a single word passing.

"Well, yes," says Cougar, "while you are fully aware of four layman dimensions, cougars are...you do know your four layman dimensions, don't you?"

"Sure," replies Bunny, "Left, right, up and down."

"Not exactly," says Cougar, "They are: height; width; depth; and time."

"Well, left, right, up and down works fine for me," says Bunny, in a huff.

"That's the point. They work fine for personal reference but they have serious limitations," Cougar replies "Let me demonstrate. Do you know where Bat's Bluff is?"

"Yes," says Bunny.

"You go there, face a bat hanging in a tree and ask him to point left. You point left at the same time. Next ask him to point right. You point right at the same time. Do the same with up and down. You will find that your directions never agree. You are both doing it from a personal reference."

"It's not my fault if the bat is incorrect," Bunny sneers.

"Just a minute," says Forester. "Your method is full of errors as well. Height, width and depth are all interchangeable depending on someone's personal reference. That is not terribly different from Bunny's idea."

"It is only an example!" says Cougar indignantly. "The point is, cougars, in fact, all cats, work in 12 dimensions… give or take a few on special physical holidays when some are closed. Cats are transporters between the four layman dimensions of the world visible to you and the 12 professional dimensions. If an animal is having difficulty in the layman dimensions, we simply help port it to three or four less demanding dimensions elsewhere. Well…actually, here for me but elsewhere for you. The poor, troubled creature is able to rest up there and return in good health and a different body to enjoy a full and natural life."

"You transform Here creatures into being There creatures?" asks Forester, upset that anyone would move a Here creature to There.

"Well, no… or, more to the point, yes," says Cougar.

Forester is shocked by this obvious mistake in clear thinking. " 'Yes' and 'no' are not interchangeable!"

"You are absolutely right, Forester," agrees Cougar "I mean, in the four layman dimensions. On the other hand, in the professional dimensions eight through 12, 'yes' and 'no' intersect…except in moral issues where they remain complete opposites."

"Okay," says Forester, "that makes sense."

"I don't understand," says Bunny, now more curious than defensive.

"That was my first point," says Cougar. "That was the one I hoped you understood. Anyway, that is why cats choose to be alone. Conversation is just too difficult. A simple 'Hello' in four dimensions turns into everything from an insult to an invitation for a lifelong relationship in 12. You have to know which dimensions are in play to know what to say."

Cougar heads off into the Woods. "I bid you good day now. If you are ever feeling tired and bored with life, I will try to be there for you."

Forester and Bunny continue walking to Crashing Waters, deep in thought.

After a long pause, Forester says, "Cougars are smarter than I thought."

"Yes, and they have nine lives, too," says Bunny.

"What do you mean, Bunny?" asks Forester.

"They are only using four dimensions in this life and they have eight more elsewhere," Bunny replies.

"Wow, Bunny! There is so much to learn! I thought there was only beardom and all the rest," says Forester, scratching his head.

"What did you think all the rest was?" asks Bunny.

"Incorrect," Forester says. "I thought everyone was incorrect but bears. I guess I thought they were like bears without beardom."

"Or bunnies without bunnyocity," laughs Bunny, hopping beside the big bear.

Wise Bear

The highway men

Forester and Bunny go and sit by the ribbon to watch ribbon runners. If they both apply their own special talents and then compare, maybe together they can understand the situation better.

"Did I ever tell you Moose has seen where they stop to gather?" Forester says reflectively.

"Go on," says Bunny.

"I am serious!" insists Forester.

"No, I mean, please do go on. I am listening," Bunny replies.

Forester explains, "Oh, well…of course…the land there is dead and all the headless turtles line up like in that place on the other side of the mountain where the flat stones covered in hieroglyphics are all in a row. Moose told me how the parasites go into caves while the Turtles sit under great sticks that chase the night away. Moose concluded the turtles and their parasites can't touch living things. A deer had seen one leave the ribbon and immediately blow up into flames. Even the big crabs that dragged it away were careful not to touch living things. Moose and Deer both guess the creatures are hypnotized or are being controlled by something other than themselves. They feel sorry for them. You know, Bunny, there is a lot in what Moose and Deer say."

"That is so true," says Bunny.

"I have come to understand," Forester says, "that many of our misunderstandings are based on a misunderstanding."

"What?" says Bunny, puzzled.

"Bear with me," Forester replies before continuing with his theory. "Differences are opportunities. Opportunities to discover. When Jacob came here, he came from a very different place. He was very different. The place he came from was loud and fast and filled with emptiness. He brought that emptiness with him and through time we filled it with friendship. He always appreciated that, but the most important thing to me is what Jacob brought to us. As he spoke of many wondrous and dangerous things we had never imagined, we became explorers. We listened and traveled on his words. We learned with our eyes closed and our minds opened. We learned that all as it is may not be as it seems. His stories protect us to this day. Had I not seen the circus clown on the flying hedge, I might not have known that it couldn't see me. Oh, it probably saw something, but it wasn't me."

Forester pauses to reflect. "All of those wonderful things happen because Jacob was different."

"I don't understand," says Bunny.

"Yes, you do, Bunny. You taught me," Forester smiles.

"I taught you something, Forester? Wow!"

"You taught me a lot, Bunny," explains Forester "You added just enough Bunny and bunnyocity to my Forester and beardom to make me understand so much better. You gave me another set of eyes with which to see the world. Not just the world, Bunny, but everything. Cougar showed me there is more everything than I ever imagined. There is no sense in my giving up being a bear to be a bunny or a cougar. I will only be a bear pretending to be a bunny or a cougar. Being Forester – a bear – is the best thing that ever happened to me. I know it well. I do it well. If things in Forester need to be changed, they need to be changed as a bear would change. Becoming a bunny will never hide my beardom. Not even from me. I am a bear because that's the way The-Way-It-Is made me. I am proud to be a bear. And proud to know a bunny."

"And I am Bunny with my best friend, Forester, because that's The-Way-It-Is made me. I am very happy to be me and even more happy to be me knowing you," says Bunny.

"Bunny, do you remember when we saw the multicolored parasites walking on their hind legs with those enormous bumps on their backs?" asks Forester.

"Please go on. I want to see what you saw," Bunny says.

"I think they are us. You know…another us. They look like us in all the basic ways. I think they are not parasites, but us's trapped in cages. I have seen belts holding them in place while studying them on the ribbon. I don't know why they would have belts. How can they enjoy the rain and the sun and the sounds and smells of the Woods? They could not possibly want to miss out on all the wonders of the Woods, could they? That's what makes me think they are trapped," says Forester.

"Maybe they lost touch with the Woods and their home and can't remember." Bunny suggests helpfully.

"I am afraid you may be correct, Bunny," replies Forester. "They may not be living in all of their four dimensions. They drive through Here like there is no Here. It is just some place between There...."

Forester points up the ribbon, then turns and points down the ribbon, "and There."

He continues, "It is like the time between thoughts. It seems not to exist

because you have no way of knowing it is there. It doesn't matter how big something is or how good it is if you don't know it is there. I am concerned for them. I don't pretend to understand them or the way they only touch stuff that is not living, but there is something about them that is us. Yes, that's it. They have an "us" quality. The ribbon runners don't have it, but the parasites or prisoners or whatever they are, do."

"Do you think the ones we saw escaped?" asks Bunny.

"Temporarily, maybe," replies Forester. "They looked happy to me. Escaping isn't happy. Maybe being here makes them happy."

"Forester, are you trying to convert There animals into Here animals?" asks Bunny.

Forester laughs. "Noooooh, Bunny, I don't think I will be doing any more of that. I am just thinking that There creatures are very much like Here creatures, but they live There and have some habits we don't yet understand."

"There creatures sound unhappy to me," says Bunny.

"I agree, Bunny. They seem to be driven by something, but what?"

"If there is nothing else, it must be themselves," concludes Bunny.

"How well we have come to know one another, Bunny," Forester says with a smile.

Spirit Bear

Bear everywhere

Many springs have come and gone when one morning Forester wakes and looks around. Once again, things are beautiful, but this time they are even more beautiful. Forester has a special sense of things now. A bigger sense. He feels a special part of everything. It is then that Forester realizes he is going to die. He tells Bunny that he is going for a long walk, but that Bunny shouldn't come this time; they will never see each other again. Bunny looks at Forester and draws a breath.

"Forester, I will see you everywhere," Bunny says softly.

"I will be gone."

"No," says Bunny, "this is an area bunnies know very well. You will be a part of everything. You will be everywhere. You are a great creature. You are a great bear. You will always be a part of everything."

"Really, Bunny?"

"You bet your bear butt! At least, everything that is good, anyway."

Forester smiles and hugs Bunny.

"In fact, Forester, I am going to call our home 'The Forest.'"

"Oh, Bunny! You are such a good friend!" Forester laughs.

"I would call it 'Forester', but there will only ever be one Forester."

"What will others think?" asks Forester.

"I know they will agree," replies Bunny.

"And if anyone doesn't?"

"They don't have to call it 'The Forest.'"

"What do you think those others will call it, Bunny?"

"Oh, I don't know," says Bunny. "If they don't know you are Here or can't see us, they may not think to call it anything. If they can't see the forest for the trees, they will probably name it...didn't Jacob tell you of places called Bald Mountain or the Golf and Country Club, maybe they will just call it

48

Theme Park or Parking Lot."

"Bunny, think of what Cougar said. You must try to understand them. Maybe they would want to be Here if they knew we were here. Not being able to see us must make it difficult. It could be a missing or malfunctioning dimension sensor," reasons Forester.

"Don't you worry, Forester. They will come home to the Woods someday. Once they can really see our beautiful home, they will return."

"Throw a pebble in the lake sometime and think of me, Bunny. Bye for now," Forester nods farewell.

Forester walks away on his favorite path. There are no more words. The two of them have grown beyond words. They have grown together. They are part of everything.

As the days come and the days go, Bunny wonders more about Forester. Everywhere Bunny looks, there is Forester. She wonders how he sees things now. She can't imagine what it is like to be everywhere at once. Bunny closes her eyes and imagines how Forester sees things. With her eyes closed, Bunny wants nothing more than to see things the way Forester does. She really wants it more than anything else.

Backstage